Susanna Tee

low fat

simple and delicious easy-to-make recipes

p

This is a Parragon Book
This edition published in 2005

Parragon
Queen Street House
4 Queen Street
Bath BA1 1HE, UK

ISBN: 1-40546-228-0

Printed in China

Produced by
THE BRIDGEWATER BOOK COMPANY LTD

Photographer Ian Parsons
Home Economist Sara Hesketh

Cover Photography Calvey Taylor-Haw
Home Economist Ruth Pollock

NOTES FOR THE READER

- The nutritional information boxes show measurements calculated per portion of food.

- This book uses both metric and imperial measurements. Follow the same units of measurement throughout; do not mix metric and imperial.

- All spoon measurements are level: teaspoons are assumed to be 5 ml, and tablespoons are assumed to be 15 ml.

- Unless otherwise stated, milk is assumed to be low fat, eggs and individual vegetables such as potatoes are medium, and pepper is freshly ground black pepper.

- Recipes using raw or very lightly cooked eggs should be avoided by infants, the elderly, pregnant women, convalescents, and anyone suffering from an illness.

- Optional ingredients, variations or serving suggestions have not been included in the calculations.

- The times given are an approximate guide only. Preparation times differ according to the techniques used by different people and the cooking times vary as a result of the type of oven used.

contents

introduction

This book will convince you that a low-fat diet need never be dreary. These healthy dishes are bursting with flavour. All are easy to prepare and good to eat. There are no complicated cooking methods involved or expensive ingredients to buy.

The recipes use fat-free or fat-reduced cooking methods, and all you need to do is to select low-fat dairy products, lean meats such as skinned chicken and turkey, and the leanest cuts of beef, lamb and pork, and of course, plenty of vegetables.

Vegetable oil spray also reduces the amount of fat used, for example when stir-frying, and non-stick liner is useful for lining baking trays. The only special equipment you need is a heavy-based, non-stick frying pan or a non-stick wok.

chicken & vegetable soup
page 12

quick-fried pork & pears
page 58

When serving bread or vegetables with these dishes, don't be tempted to reach for the butter dish. Simply eat delicious fresh bread on its own and add a generous sprinkling of chopped herbs to the vegetables. Instead of buying very rich salad dressings, you can make your own using low-fat yogurt or fromage frais, or use a fat-reduced mayonnaise. You will soon be feeling healthier without feeling deprived of your favourite dishes.

easy

Recipes are graded as follows:
1 spoon = easy;
2 spoons = very easy;
3 spoons = extremely easy.

serves 4

Recipes generally serve four people. Simply halve the ingredients to serve two, taking care not to mix metric and imperial measurements.

15 minutes

Preparation time. Where marinating or soaking are involved, these times have been added on separately: eg, 15 minutes + 30 minutes to marinate.

40 minutes

Cooking time. Cooking times do not include the cooking of side dishes or accompaniments served with the main dishes.

penne primavera
page 68

apple & honey water ice
page 90

These are recipes that are easy to make yet satisfying to eat at a midday break or as a light evening meal. They are ideal served simply with fresh crusty bread and then followed with fresh fruit for a low-fat, healthy lunch or supper. Most of them – for example, Sweet Red Pepper & Tomato Soup, and Greek Feta Salad – can also be served as a starter as they are light and refreshing. Choose from delicious temptations such as Chilled Smoked Mackerel with Horseradish Dressing, Prawn & Mango Salad and Vegetable Frittata.

light lunches
& suppers

sweet red pepper & tomato soup

extremely easy

serves 4

5 minutes

30–35 minutes

ingredients

1 tbsp olive oil

2 tbsp water

2 red peppers, cored, deseeded
    and chopped finely

1 garlic clove, chopped finely

1 onion, chopped finely

400 g/14 oz canned chopped tomatoes

1.2 litres/2 pints vegetable stock

salt and pepper

fresh basil leaves, to garnish

NUTRITIONAL INFORMATION	
calories	89
protein	3 g
carbohydrate	12 g
sugars	10 g
fat	4 g
saturates	0.5 g

Put the oil, water, peppers, garlic and onion in a saucepan, heat gently and cook for 5–10 minutes, or until the vegetables have softened. Cover the pan and simmer for a further 10 minutes.

Add the tomatoes, stock, salt and pepper and simmer, uncovered, for 15 minutes.

Serve garnished with basil leaves.

mixed bean soup

extremely easy

serves 4

10 minutes

35 minutes

ingredients

1 garlic clove, crushed
1 onion, chopped finely
1 celery stalk, sliced finely
1 carrot, diced finely
1 leek, sliced finely
400 g/14 oz canned chopped tomatoes
600 ml/1 pint vegetable stock

salt and pepper
pinch of dried mixed herbs
400 g/14 oz canned red kidney beans,
    drained
400 g/14 oz black-eyed beans, drained

warm crusty bread, to serve

NUTRITIONAL INFORMATION	
calories	238
protein	16 g
carbohydrate	42 g
sugars	11 g
fat	2 g
saturates	neg

Put all the ingredients, except the beans, into a large saucepan. Bring to the boil, then simmer for 30 minutes, stirring from time to time, until the vegetables are tender.

Add the beans and simmer for a further 4–5 minutes, or until hot.

Serve with warm crusty bread.

chicken & vegetable soup

extremely easy

serves 4

10 minutes

1 hour 10 minutes

ingredients

1 onion, chopped finely
1 garlic clove, chopped finely
115 g/4 oz white cabbage, shredded
2 medium carrots, chopped finely
4 potatoes, diced
1 green pepper, cored, deseeded and diced
400 g/14 oz canned chopped tomatoes

1.3 litres/2¼ pints chicken stock
salt and pepper
175 g/6 oz cooked chicken, diced

chopped fresh parsley, to garnish

warm crusty bread, to serve

NUTRITIONAL INFORMATION	
calories	240
protein	19 g
carbohydrate	37 g
sugars	10 g
fat	3 g
saturates	0.5 g

Put all the ingredients, except the chicken and parsley, in a large saucepan and bring to the boil. Simmer for 1 hour, or until the vegetables are tender.

Add the chicken and simmer for a further 10 minutes, or until hot.

Garnish with parsley and serve with warm crusty bread.

tuna & fresh vegetable salad

extremely easy   serves 4

10 minutes + 1 hour to marinate   none

ingredients

DRESSING
4 tbsp reduced-calorie mayonnaise
4 tbsp low-fat natural yogurt
2 tbsp white wine vinegar
salt and pepper

12 cherry tomatoes, halved
225 g/8 oz whole green beans, cut into
   2.5 cm/1 inch pieces

225 g/8 oz courgettes, sliced thinly
225 g/8 oz button mushrooms,
   sliced thinly
350 g/12 oz canned tuna in brine, drained
   and flaked

chopped fresh parsley, to garnish

salad leaves, to serve

NUTRITIONAL INFORMATION	
calories	187
protein	26 g
carbohydrate	8 g
sugars	7 g
fat	6 g
saturates	0.5 g

To make the dressing, put the mayonnaise, yogurt, vinegar, salt and pepper in a screw-topped jar and shake together until the ingredients are well blended.

Put the tomatoes, beans, courgettes and mushrooms in a bowl. Pour over the dressing and leave to marinate for about 1 hour.

To serve, arrange the salad leaves on a serving dish. Add the vegetables and then the tuna and garnish with chopped parsley.

greek feta salad

extremely easy

serves 4

10 minutes

ingredients

DRESSING
3 tbsp extra virgin olive oil
1 tbsp lemon juice
½ tsp dried oregano
salt and pepper

4 tomatoes, sliced
½ cucumber, peeled and sliced

1 small red onion, sliced thinly
115 g/4 oz feta cheese (drained weight),
    cubed
8 black olives

a few vine leaves, to serve

NUTRITIONAL INFORMATION	
calories	186
protein	6 g
carbohydrate	7 g
sugars	6 g
fat	15 g
saturates	5 g

To make the dressing, put the oil, lemon juice, oregano, salt and pepper in a screw-topped jar and shake together until blended.

Arrange the vine leaves on a serving dish and then the tomatoes, cucumber and onion. Scatter the cheese and olives on top. Pour the dressing over the salad and serve.

prawn & mango salad

extremely easy · serves 4

10 minutes · none

NUTRITIONAL INFORMATION

calories	146
protein	16 g
carbohydrate	15 g
sugars	14 g
fat	3 g
saturates	0.5 g

ingredients

2 mangoes
225 g/8 oz peeled, cooked prawns

DRESSING
juice from the mangoes
6 tbsp low-fat natural yogurt
2 tbsp reduced-calorie mayonnaise
1 tbsp lemon juice
salt and pepper

salad leaves, to serve

4 whole cooked prawns, to garnish

Cutting close to the stone, cut a large slice from one side of each mango, then cut another slice from the opposite side. Without breaking the skin, cut the flesh in the segments into squares, then push the skin inside out to expose the cubes and cut away from the skin. Use a sharp knife to peel the remaining centre section and cut the flesh away from the stone into cubes. Reserve any juice in a bowl and put the mango flesh in a separate bowl.

Add the prawns to the mango flesh. To the juice, add the yogurt, mayonnaise, lemon juice, salt and pepper and blend together.

Arrange the salad leaves on a serving dish and add the mango flesh and prawns. Pour over the dressing and serve garnished with the whole prawns.

warm chicken liver salad

very easy   serves 4

5 minutes   10–12 minutes

ingredients

salad leaves
1 tbsp olive oil
1 small onion, chopped finely
450 g/1 lb frozen chicken livers, thawed

1 tsp chopped fresh tarragon
1 tsp wholegrain mustard
2 tbsp balsamic vinegar
salt and pepper

NUTRITIONAL INFORMATION	
calories	142
protein	21 g
carbohydrate	2 g
sugars	1 g
fat	6 g
saturates	1 g

Arrange the salad leaves on serving plates.

Heat the oil in a non-stick frying pan, add the onion and cook for 5 minutes, or until softened. Add the chicken livers, tarragon and mustard and cook for 3–5 minutes, stirring, until tender. Put on top of the salad leaves.

Add the vinegar, salt and pepper to the pan and heat, stirring all the time, until all the sediment has been lifted from the pan. Pour over the chicken livers and serve warm.

chilled smoked mackerel
with horseradish dressing

extremely easy   serves 4

10 minutes + at least 30 minutes to chill   none

4 smoked mackerel

watercress sprigs, to garnish

DRESSING
150 ml/5 fl oz low-fat natural yogurt
1 tsp grated horseradish
salt and pepper

NUTRITIONAL INFORMATION	
calories	376
protein	21 g
carbohydrate	3 g
sugars	3 g
fat	31 g
saturates	6 g

Remove the skin from the mackerel fillets, then cut each fillet in half lengthways. Chill in the refrigerator for at least 30 minutes.

Meanwhile, mix together the yogurt, horseradish, salt and pepper. Chill in the refrigerator with the mackerel.

To serve, arrange the mackerel on serving plates, spoon over the horseradish dressing and garnish with watercress sprigs.

vegetable frittata

easy   serves 4

10 minutes   20–30
minutes

ingredients

4 whole eggs
2 egg whites
salt and pepper
1 tsp olive oil
1 onion, chopped roughly
1 garlic clove, chopped finely
1 green pepper, deseeded, cored and
   chopped finely

1 courgette, sliced thickly
225 g/8 oz cooked potatoes, diced
1 tomato, chopped roughly
55 g/2 oz reduced-fat mozzarella cheese,
   grated

NUTRITIONAL INFORMATION	
calories	215
protein	13 g
carbohydrate	15 g
sugars	5 g
fat	12 g
saturates	4 g

Beat the whole eggs and egg whites in a bowl and season with salt and pepper.

Heat the oil in a large non-stick frying pan and add the onion, garlic and green pepper. Cook for 5 minutes, or until softened. Add the courgette and potatoes and cook for a further 5–10 minutes, or until lightly browned. Stir in the tomato.

Pour in the egg mixture and cook over a low heat for 5–10 minutes, or until the mixture is set and only the top is runny. Sprinkle the cheese over the top.

Transfer the pan to a preheated grill and cook until the top is set but not hard and the cheese has melted and begun to brown. Serve hot, cut into wedges.

home-made turkey burgers

easy   serves 8

15 minutes   20 minutes

55 g/2 oz long-grain white rice
salt and pepper
450 g/1 lb lean minced turkey
1 small cooking apple, peeled, cored and
    grated
1 small onion, chopped finely

1 garlic clove, chopped finely
1 tsp ground sage
½ tsp dried thyme
½ tsp ground allspice
vegetable oil spray, for frying

NUTRITIONAL INFORMATION	
calories	161
protein	26 g
carbohydrate	10 g
sugars	5 g
fat	2 g
saturates	1 g

Cook the rice in a large pan of boiling salted water for about 10 minutes, or until tender. Drain, rinse under cold running water, then drain well again.

Put the cooked rice and all the remaining ingredients in a large bowl and mix well together. With wet hands, shape the mixture into 8 thick burgers.

Spray a large non-stick frying pan with oil, add the burgers and cook for about 10 minutes, turning them over several times, until they are golden brown. Remove from the pan and serve while hot.

The following recipes show just how easy it is to prepare low-fat dishes. They all use lean cuts of meat, poultry and fish that are seasoned with fresh vegetables, herbs and spices, and are packed with flavour. There are recipes for family meals and entertaining, and recipes for warm summer evenings or cold winter nights. Choose from such dishes as Moussaka, Chicken with a Honey-glazed Crust, Marinated Lamb Kebabs, and Grilled Salmon with Red Pepper Sauce. All are mouthwatering – the only difficulty is deciding which to choose!

main courses

mexican chicken burritos

very easy   serves 4

10 minutes   30 minutes

ingredients

8 wheat flour tortillas
vegetable oil spray
1 onion, chopped finely
4 boneless chicken breasts, skinned and
    sliced thinly

1 packet taco seasoning
4 tomatoes, chopped roughly
4 spring onions, sliced finely

1 tub tomato salsa, to serve

NUTRITIONAL INFORMATION	
calories	473
protein	40 g
carbohydrate	75 g
sugars	7 g
fat	4 g
saturates	1 g

Preheat the oven to 150°C/300°F/Gas Mark 2.

Wrap the tortillas in aluminium foil and cook in the oven for 10 minutes, or until soft.

Meanwhile, spray a large non-stick frying pan with oil. Add the onion and cook for 5 minutes, or until softened. Add the chicken. Stirring occasionally, cook for 5 minutes, or until tender. Stir in the taco seasoning.

Preheat the oven to 180°C/350°F/Gas Mark 4. Put the chicken mixture in the centre of each tortilla and add the tomatoes and spring onions. Fold the tortillas into a parcel and put in an ovenproof dish.

Cover the dish and cook in the preheated oven for 20 minutes. Spoon the tomato salsa over the hot tortillas before serving.

chicken with a honey-glazed crust

very easy   serves 4

5 minutes   30–40
minutes

ingredients

3 tbsp wheat germ

3 tbsp honey

1 tbsp French mustard

4 chicken breasts, skinned

green salad, to serve

NUTRITIONAL INFORMATION	
calories	194
protein	31 g
carbohydrate	13 g
sugars	12 g
fat	2 g
saturates	0.5 g

Preheat the oven to 190°C/375°F/Gas Mark 5.

Put the wheat germ, honey and mustard in a bowl and mix well together.
Put the chicken breasts on a baking sheet and spread with the honey mixture.

Bake the chicken in the oven for 30–40 minutes, or until the chicken is tender and
a crust has formed. Remove from the oven and transfer to warm serving dishes.

Serve with green salad, if desired.

italian braised chicken & fennel

very easy   serves 4

5 minutes   35 minutes

4 tomatoes, chopped finely
1 garlic clove, crushed
50 ml/2 fl oz white wine
2 tsp balsamic vinegar
salt and pepper

4 chicken breasts, skinned
4 small fennel bulbs, quartered

flat-leaved parsley, to garnish

NUTRITIONAL INFORMATION	
calories	166
protein	32 g
carbohydrate	5 g
sugars	5 g
fat	2 g
saturates	0.5 g

Put the tomatoes, garlic, wine, vinegar, salt and pepper in a large non-stick frying pan and bring to the boil. Reduce the heat and add the chicken and fennel pieces. Cover and simmer for about 30 minutes, or until the chicken and fennel are tender.

Using a draining spoon, transfer the chicken and fennel to warmed serving plates.

Bring the sauce back to the boil and cook, stirring occasionally, until thickened slightly. Spoon the sauce over the chicken and serve garnished with parsley.

tandoori chicken

very easy   serves 4

10 minutes
+ 24 hours
to marinate

45 minutes
to 1 hour

ingredients

4–8 chicken portions, skinned

MARINADE
1 small onion, quartered
2 garlic cloves
1 tsp chopped fresh ginger
2 tsp ground cumin
2 tsp ground coriander

1 tsp garam masala
½ tsp salt
½ tsp cayenne pepper, optional
2 tbsp lemon or lime juice
4 tbsp low-fat natural yogurt
¼ tsp red food colouring

lemon or lime wedges, to garnish

NUTRITIONAL INFORMATION	
calories	160
protein	50 g
carbohydrate	4 g
sugars	3 g
fat	20 g
saturates	1 g

Using a sharp knife, cut 1-cm/½-inch deep slashes in each piece of chicken and put in a shallow dish.

Put all the remaining ingredients in a food processor and blend until smooth. Spread the marinade over the chicken pieces, working it into the cuts in the flesh. Cover the dish and marinate in the refrigerator for 24 hours.

Preheat the oven to 200°C/400°F/Gas Mark 6.

Place the chicken pieces on a rack in a roasting tin and cook in the oven for 45 minutes to 1 hour, turning the pieces over once and basting with the juices in the tin, until tender.

Serve garnished with lemon or lime wedges.

herb-crusted haddock with tomato salsa

very easy   serves 4

10 minutes   10–15
             minutes

ingredients

115 g/4 oz fresh white breadcrumbs
3 tbsp lemon juice
1 tbsp pesto sauce
2 tbsp chopped fresh parsley
salt and pepper

vegetable oil spray
4 haddock fillets

1 tub tomato salsa, to serve

NUTRITIONAL INFORMATION	
calories	245
protein	41 g
carbohydrate	16 g
sugars	2 g
fat	2 g
saturates	0 g

Put the breadcrumbs, 2 tablespoons of the lemon juice, the pesto sauce, parsley, salt and pepper in a bowl and mix well together.

Line a grill pan with aluminium foil and spray with vegetable oil. Place the haddock fillets on the foil and sprinkle with the remaining tablespoon of lemon juice, more salt and pepper and cook under a preheated grill for 5 minutes.

Turn the haddock fillets over and spread the herb and breadcrumb mixture over the top of each.

Cook for a further 5–10 minutes, or until the haddock is tender and the crust is golden brown.

Serve with the tomato salsa spooned over the top of each fish.

grilled salmon with red pepper sauce

easy   serves 4

15 minutes   35–45 minutes

ingredients

3 red peppers, whole
vegetable oil spray
4 salmon steaks
1 tbsp lemon juice
salt and pepper

1 onion, chopped finely
1 garlic clove, chopped finely
2 tsp balsamic vinegar
handful of fresh basil leaves

NUTRITIONAL INFORMATION	
calories	326
protein	32 g
carbohydrate	11 g
sugars	10 g
fat	17 g
saturates	3 g

Preheat the oven to 200°C/400°F/Gas Mark 6.

Put the peppers on a baking sheet and roast in the oven for 25 minutes, turning once, until deflated and slightly charred. Leave to cool, then peel off the skin and discard with the core and seeds.

Meanwhile, line a grill pan with aluminium foil and spray with oil. Place the salmon steaks on the foil, sprinkle with lemon juice, salt and pepper and cook under a preheated grill for 10–20 minutes, turning once, until tender.

Spray a small non-stick saucepan with oil and fry the onion and garlic for 5 minutes, or until softened. Blend in a food processor with the pepper flesh, vinegar, basil, salt and pepper until smooth. Return the mixture to the pan and reheat gently.

Serve the red pepper sauce with the cooked salmon steaks.

baked fish & chips

very easy   serves 4

20 minutes   40–45
minutes

450 g/1 lb floury potatoes, peeled and cut
  into thick, even-sized chips
vegetable oil spray
55 g/2 oz plain white flour

1 egg
55 g/2 oz fresh white breadcrumbs,
  seasoned with salt and pepper
4 cod or haddock fillets

NUTRITIONAL INFORMATION	
calories	322
protein	37 g
carbohydrate	37 g
sugars	1 g
fat	4 g
saturates	1 g

Preheat the oven to 200°C/400°F/Gas Mark 6. Line 2 baking sheets with non-stick liner.

Rinse the chipped potatoes under cold running water, then dry well on a clean tea towel. Put in a bowl, spray with oil and toss together until coated. Spread the chips on a baking sheet and cook in the oven for 40–45 minutes, turning once, until golden.

Meanwhile, put the flour on a plate, beat the egg in a shallow dish and spread the seasoned breadcrumbs on a large plate. Dip the fish fillets in the flour to coat, then the egg, allowing any excess to drip off, and finally the breadcrumbs, patting them firmly into the fish. Place the fish in one layer on a baking sheet.

Fifteen minutes before the chips have cooked, bake the fish fillets in the oven for 10–15 minutes, turning them once during cooking, until the fish is tender. Serve the fish with the chips.

red mullet with citrus fruit

very easy   serves 4

10 minutes   10–15
+ 4 hours   minutes
to marinate

ingredients

MARINADE
6 tbsp fresh orange juice
3 tbsp lemon juice
3 tbsp lime juice
4 tbsp dry sherry
1 tsp chopped garlic
1 tsp chopped ginger
salt and pepper

vegetable oil spray, for frying
4 red mullet

orange segments, to garnish

NUTRITIONAL
INFORMATION

calories	194
protein	28 g
carbohydrate	3 g
sugars	3 g
fat	6 g
saturates	0 g

Put all the marinade ingredients in a shallow dish and mix them well together.

Using a sharp knife, slash the mullet three times on each side. Add the fish to the marinade and leave to marinate in the refrigerator, turning once or twice, for about 4 hours.

Line a grill pan with aluminium foil and spray with vegetable oil. Place the fish on the foil and cook under a preheated grill for 10–15 minutes, turning once and spooning over the marinade, until the flesh is tender.

Serve garnished with orange segments.

plaice parcels with fresh herbs

very easy   serves 4

10 minutes   15 minutes

ingredients

vegetable oil spray
4 plaice fillets, skinned
6 tbsp chopped fresh herbs, such as dill,
   parsley, chives, thyme or marjoram

finely grated zest and juice of 2 lemons
1 small onion, sliced thinly
1 tbsp capers, optional
salt and pepper

NUTRITIONAL INFORMATION	
calories	129
protein	25 g
carbohydrate	2 g
sugars	1 g
fat	2 g
saturates	0 g

Preheat the oven to 190°C/375°F/Gas Mark 5. Cut 4 large squares of aluminium foil, each large enough to hold a fish and form a parcel, and spray with oil.

Place each fish fillet on a foil sheet and sprinkle over the herbs, lemon rind and juice, onion, capers (if using), salt and pepper. Fold the foil to make a secure parcel and place on a baking sheet.

Bake the parcels in the oven for 15 minutes, or until tender.

Serve the fish piping hot, in their loosely opened parcels.

stir-fried beef & mangetouts

very easy   serves 4

10 minutes   10 minutes

ingredients

450 g/1 lb rump or sirloin steak,
    sliced thinly
2 tbsp soy sauce
5 tbsp hoisin sauce
2 tbsp dry sherry
vegetable oil spray
1 onion, sliced thinly
1 tsp chopped fresh garlic
1 tsp chopped fresh ginger

1 carrot, sliced thinly
450 g/1 lb mangetouts
225 g/8 oz canned sliced bamboo shoots,
    drained

fresh sprigs of coriander, to garnish

cooked rice or noodles, to serve

NUTRITIONAL INFORMATION	
calories	249
protein	33 g
carbohydrate	15 g
sugars	12 g
fat	6 g
saturates	2 g

Put the strips of beef in a bowl, add the soy sauce, hoisin sauce and sherry and stir together. Leave to marinate while cooking the vegetables.

Spray a large non-stick wok with oil. Add the onion, garlic, ginger, carrot and mangetouts and stir-fry for 5 minutes, or until softened.

Add the beef and marinade to the wok and stir-fry for 2–3 minutes, or until tender. Add the bamboo shoots and stir-fry for a further minute, until hot.

Transfer to a warm serving dish, garnish with coriander and serve with cooked rice or noodles, if desired.

bœuf stroganoff

very easy   serves 4

5 minutes   15 minutes

vegetable oil spray
1 onion, sliced roughly
225 g/8 oz button mushrooms, sliced thinly
1 tsp French mustard
450 g/1 lb rump or sirloin steak,
   sliced thinly

300 ml/10 fl oz reduced-fat crème fraîche
salt and pepper

chopped fresh parsley, to garnish

NUTRITIONAL INFORMATION	
calories	302
protein	30 g
carbohydrate	7 g
sugars	5 g
fat	17 g
saturates	11 g

Spray a large, non-stick frying pan with oil. Add the onion and cook, stirring, for 5 minutes, until softened and lightly coloured.

Add the mushrooms and mustard to the pan and fry, stirring occasionally, for a further 4–5 minutes, or until lightly coloured.

Add the beef to the pan and fry, stirring occasionally, for 5 minutes, or until tender. Add the crème fraîche and salt and pepper, then heat, stirring all the time, until hot.

Serve garnished with chopped parsley.

linguine with prawns

very easy   serves 4

5 minutes   15 minutes

ingredients

350 g/12 oz linguine
salt and pepper
1 tbsp white wine vinegar
1 tbsp lemon juice
2 tbsp tomato purée
pinch of sugar
6 tbsp water

1 tsp chopped fresh garlic
1 tsp chopped fresh ginger
225 g/8 oz shelled cooked prawns
4 spring onions, sliced thinly

chopped fresh parsley, to garnish

NUTRITIONAL INFORMATION	
calories	359
protein	21 g
carbohydrate	68 g
sugars	5 g
fat	2 g
saturates	0 g

Cook the pasta in a large saucepan of boiling salted water for 10 minutes, or as directed on the packet, until tender.

Meanwhile, put the vinegar, lemon juice, tomato purée, sugar, water, salt and pepper in a bowl and mix together.

Put the garlic, ginger, prawns and spring onions in a large non-stick frying pan and heat for 1–2 minutes, stirring all the time, until hot.

Drain the cooked pasta and add to the frying pan. Mix into the sauce mixture and heat, stirring, until the pasta is well coated and the sauce is heated through.

Serve garnished with chopped parsley.

moussaka

easy   serves 4

40 minutes   45 minutes

ingredients

2 aubergines, sliced thinly
450 g/1 lb lean minced beef
2 onions, sliced finely
1 tsp finely chopped garlic
400 g/14 oz canned tomatoes

2 tbsp chopped fresh parsley
salt and pepper
2 eggs
300 ml/10 fl oz low-fat natural yogurt
1 tbsp grated Parmesan cheese

NUTRITIONAL INFORMATION	
calories	357
protein	36 g
carbohydrate	17 g
sugars	15 g
fat	16 g
saturates	7 g

In a large non-stick frying pan, dry-fry the aubergine slices, in batches, on both sides until brown. Remove from the pan.

Add the beef to the pan and cook for 5 minutes, stirring, until browned. Stir in the onions and garlic and cook for 5 minutes, or until lightly browned. Add the tomatoes, parsley, salt and pepper, then bring the mixture to the boil and simmer for 20 minutes, or until the meat is tender.

Preheat the oven to 180°C/350°F/Gas Mark 4. Arrange half the aubergine slices in a layer in an ovenproof dish. Add the meat mixture, then a final layer of the remaining aubergine slices.

In a bowl, beat the eggs, then beat in the yogurt and add salt and pepper. Pour the mixture over the aubergines and sprinkle the grated cheese on top. Bake the moussaka in the oven for 45 minutes, or until golden brown. Serve straight from the dish.

marinated lamb kebabs

very easy   serves 4

10 minutes   15–20
+ 2–3 hours   minutes
to marinate

MARINADE
150 ml/5 fl oz low-fat natural yogurt
4 tbsp chopped fresh coriander
2 tsp chopped garlic
2 tsp chopped ginger
1 tsp ground coriander
1 tsp ground cumin
salt and pepper

450 g/1 lb leg of lamb, cut into 2.5-cm/
   1-inch cubes

chopped fresh parsley, to garnish

salad, to serve

NUTRITIONAL INFORMATION	
calories	200
protein	25 g
carbohydrate	3 g
sugars	3 g
fat	10 g
saturates	4 g

Put all the marinade ingredients into a large bowl and mix together. Stir in the lamb until coated in the marinade, then leave to marinate in the refrigerator for 2–3 hours.

Thread the lamb cubes onto metal or bamboo skewers. Cook under a preheated grill for 15–20 minutes, turning frequently and basting with the marinade, until tender.

Garnish with chopped parsley and serve with salad.

quick-fried pork & pears

very easy   serves 4

15 minutes 5–7 minutes

ingredients

1 tbsp soy sauce
1 tsp white wine vinegar
2 tbsp dry sherry
450 g/1 lb pork fillet, sliced very thinly

2 large pears
4 spring onions, sliced thinly
1 tsp chopped garlic
1 tbsp chopped ginger

NUTRITIONAL INFORMATION	
calories	210
protein	25 g
carbohydrate	9 g
sugars	8 g
fat	7 g
saturates	2 g

Put the soy sauce, vinegar and sherry in a large bowl. Add the pork and mix together. Cut the pears into 5-mm/¼-inch slices, discarding the cores.

Reserve the green part of the onions to use as garnish. Put the garlic, ginger and spring onions in a large non-stick wok and heat for 1–2 minutes, stirring all the time, until hot.

Add the pork mixture to the pan and stir-fry for 3–4 minutes, or until tender and beginning to brown. Add the pears and stir-fry for a further minute, or until hot.

Serve the stir-fry at once, sprinkled with the sliced green spring onion stems.

Vegetables are the perfect low-fat food and in this section is a collection of recipes using just vegetables as a main course. They illustrate how interesting and varied vegetables can be, but fortunately you don't have to be a vegetarian to enjoy them! You will find low-fat recipes for Cheese & Spinach Lasagne, Vegetable Biryani, Glazed Vegetable Kebabs and Stuffed Aubergines, among other delicious dishes. Their flavour and freshness have been brought out to the full to provide nutritious and satisfying meals.

vegetarian
dishes

spring vegetable risotto

easy   serves 4

15 minutes   30–35 minutes

ingredients

850 ml/1½ pints vegetable stock
2 tsp olive oil
1 small leek, sliced finely
1 tsp chopped garlic
1 carrot, sliced thinly
2 courgettes, sliced thinly
55 g/2 oz mangetouts

55 g/2 oz whole green beans, cut into
   2.5-cm/1-inch pieces
350 g/12 oz arborio rice
150 ml/5 fl oz dry white wine
55 g/2 oz frozen petits pois, thawed
salt and pepper

NUTRITIONAL INFORMATION	
calories	429
protein	10 g
carbohydrate	36 g
sugars	14 g
fat	16 g
saturates	9 g

Pour the stock into a saucepan, bring to the boil, then keep at barely simmering point.

Meanwhile, heat the oil in a non-stick saucepan, add the leek, garlic, carrot, courgettes, mangetouts and beans and cook, stirring frequently, for 5 minutes, or until beginning to soften but not brown.

Add the rice and stir well for 2–3 minutes, or until coated in the oil. Add the wine and cook, stirring, until almost evaporated.

Add about 150 ml/5 fl oz of the stock and cook gently, stirring occasionally, until absorbed. Add more stock, in 150-ml/5-fl oz measures, as soon as each measure has been absorbed, stirring frequently. Continue until the rice is thick, creamy and tender. This will take 20–25 minutes. Stir in the peas, season with salt and pepper and serve.

cheese & spinach lasagne

very easy   serves 4

15 minutes   45–50
minutes

ingredients

450 g/1 lb frozen spinach, thawed
salt and pepper
450 g/1 lb low-fat ricotta cheese
8 sheets no-precook lasagne
500 ml/18 fl oz passata (Italian tomato
  sauce)

225 g/8 oz reduced-fat mozzarella cheese,
  sliced thinly
1 tbsp Parmesan cheese

salad (optional), to serve

NUTRITIONAL INFORMATION	
calories	369
protein	23 g
carbohydrate	36 g
sugars	14 g
fat	16 g
saturates	9 g

Preheat the oven to 180°C/350°F/Gas Mark 4.

Put the spinach in a sieve and squeeze out any excess liquid. Put half in the bottom of an ovenproof dish and add salt and pepper.

Spread half the ricotta over the spinach, cover with half the lasagne sheets, then spoon over half the passata. Arrange half the mozzarella slices on top. Repeat the layers and finally sprinkle over the Parmesan cheese.

Bake in the oven for 45–50 minutes, by which time the top should be brown and bubbling.

Serve with salad, if desired.

pasta with ricotta & sun-dried tomatoes

very easy   serves 4

10 minutes   10 minutes

ingredients

350 g/12 oz tagliatelle
salt and pepper
115 g/4 oz sun-dried tomatoes in oil,
   drained
400 g/14 oz low-fat ricotta cheese
1 garlic clove, crushed

GARNISH
freshly grated Parmesan cheese
fresh basil leaves

NUTRITIONAL INFORMATION	
calories	542
protein	18 g
carbohydrate	74 g
sugars	8 g
fat	22 g
saturates	6 g

Cook the pasta in a large saucepan of boiling salted water for 10 minutes or as directed on the packet, or until tender.

Meanwhile, using scissors, cut the tomatoes into small pieces into a saucepan. Add the ricotta, garlic, salt and pepper and heat very gently, without boiling.

Drain the pasta, add to the tomato mixture and toss together.

Serve garnished with basil leaves and generously sprinkled with freshly grated Parmesan.

penne primavera

very easy   serves 4

10 minutes   20 minutes

ingredients

115 g/4 oz baby sweetcorn
115 g/4 oz whole baby carrots
salt and pepper
175 g/6 oz shelled broad beans
175 g/6 oz whole green beans, cut into
  2.5-cm/1-inch pieces

350 g/12 oz penne
300 ml/10 fl oz low-fat natural yogurt
1 tbsp chopped fresh parsley
1 tbsp snipped fresh chives

a few chives, to garnish

NUTRITIONAL INFORMATION	
calories	398
protein	19 g
carbohydrate	79 g
sugars	11 g
fat	3 g
saturates	1 g

Cook the sweetcorn and carrots in boiling salted water for 5 minutes, or until tender, then drain and rinse under cold running water. Cook the broad beans and green beans in boiling salted water for 3–4 minutes, or until tender, then drain and rinse under cold running water. If preferred, slip the skins off the broad beans.

Cook the pasta in a large saucepan of boiling salted water for 10 minutes or as directed on the packet, until tender.

Meanwhile, put the yogurt, parsley, snipped chives, salt and pepper in a bowl and mix together.

Drain the cooked pasta and return to the pan. Add the vegetables and yogurt sauce, heat gently and toss together, until hot.

Serve garnished with a few lengths of chives.

vegetable biryani

very easy   serves 4

10 minutes   30 minutes

ingredients

1 onion, quartered

2 garlic cloves

1 tsp chopped ginger

1 tsp ground coriander

1 tsp ground cumin

1 tsp ground turmeric

½ tsp chilli powder

salt and pepper

1.4 litres/2½ pints water

2 carrots, sliced thickly

225 g/8 oz whole green beans, cut into 2.5-cm/1-inch lengths

½ cauliflower head, cut into florets

350 g/12 oz basmati rice

2 whole cloves

¼ tsp cardamom seeds

2 tbsp lime juice

chopped fresh coriander, to garnish

NUTRITIONAL INFORMATION	
calories	378
protein	11 g
carbohydrate	80 g
sugars	8 g
fat	2 g
saturates	0 g

Put the onion, garlic, ginger, coriander, cumin, turmeric, chilli, salt and pepper in a food processor and blend until smooth.

Spoon the spice mixture into a large non-stick saucepan and cook, stirring, for 2 minutes. Stir in 850 ml/1½ pints of the water and bring to the boil. Add the carrots, beans and cauliflower and simmer for 15 minutes, or until tender.

Meanwhile, put the rice in a sieve and rinse under cold running water. Put in a saucepan with the remaining 600 ml/1 pint of water, the cloves, cardamom seeds and salt. Bring to the boil, then simmer for 10 minutes, or until just tender.

Drain the rice and stir into the vegetables with the lime juice. Simmer gently until the rice is tender and the liquid has been absorbed. Serve garnished with coriander.

bean & vegetable chilli

very easy   serves 4

10 minutes   20 minutes

4 tbsp vegetable stock
1 onion, chopped roughly
1 green pepper, cored, deseeded and
   chopped finely
1 red pepper, cored, deseeded and chopped
   finely
1 tsp garlic, chopped finely
1 tsp ginger, chopped finely
2 tsp ground cumin
½ tsp chilli powder

2 tbsp tomato purée
400 g/14 oz canned chopped tomatoes
salt and pepper
400 g/14 oz canned kidney beans, drained
400 g/14 oz canned black-eyed beans,
   drained

chopped fresh coriander, to garnish

fresh crusty bread, to serve

NUTRITIONAL INFORMATION	
calories	246
protein	17 g
carbohydrate	44 g
sugars	14 g
fat	2 g
saturates	0 g

Heat the stock in a large saucepan, add the onion and peppers and simmer for
5 minutes, or until softened.

Stir in the garlic, ginger, cumin, chilli powder, tomato purée, tomatoes (together
with their juice), salt and pepper, and simmer for 10 minutes. Stir in the beans and
simmer for a further 5 minutes, or until hot. Remove the pan from the heat and
transfer the chilli to a warm serving dish.

Garnish with chopped coriander and serve with fresh crusty bread.

glazed vegetable kebabs

very easy   serves 4

15 minutes   10 minutes

ingredients

150 ml/5 fl oz low-fat natural yogurt
4 tbsp mango chutney
1 tsp chopped garlic
1 tbsp lemon juice
salt and pepper
8 baby onions, peeled

16 baby sweetcorn, halved
2 courgettes, cut into 2.5-cm/1-inch pieces
16 button mushrooms
16 cherry tomatoes

mixed salad leaves, to garnish

NUTRITIONAL INFORMATION	
calories	144
protein	8 g
carbohydrate	26 g
sugars	24 g
fat	1 g
saturates	0 g

Put the yogurt, chutney, garlic, lemon juice, salt and pepper in a bowl and stir together.

Put the onions in a saucepan of boiling water. Return to the boil, then drain well.

Thread the onions, sweetcorn, courgettes, mushrooms and tomatoes alternately onto 8 metal or bamboo skewers.

Arrange the kebabs on a grill pan and brush with the yogurt glaze. Cook under a preheated grill for 10 minutes, turning and brushing frequently, until golden and tender.

Serve with a garnish of mixed salad leaves.

stuffed aubergines

easy   serves 4

15 minutes   45 minutes

2 aubergines

1 onion, chopped finely

1 tsp chopped garlic

115 g/4 oz button mushrooms, chopped
  roughly

2 tsp chopped fresh coriander

55 g/2 oz fresh breadcrumbs

salt and pepper

55 g/2 oz feta cheese (drained weight),
  crumbled finely

NUTRITIONAL INFORMATION	
calories	104
protein	5 g
carbohydrate	13 g
sugars	5 g
fat	4 g
saturates	2 g

Put the aubergines in a large saucepan of boiling water and cook for 20 minutes, or until tender. Drain well.

Cut the aubergines in half lengthways, scoop out the flesh and chop finely. Reserve the aubergine shells.

Preheat the oven to 180°C/350°F/Gas Mark 4.

Put the aubergine flesh, onion, garlic, mushrooms and coriander in a non-stick frying pan and cook for 5 minutes. Stir in the breadcrumbs, salt and pepper.

Stuff the aubergine shells with the mixture and sprinkle with the feta cheese.

Place on a baking sheet and bake in the oven for 20 minutes. Transfer to warm serving plates and serve immediately.

The low-fat pudding and dessert recipes in this chapter use fresh or dried fruits and are bursting with tempting flavours. There is a selection of both hot puddings and cold desserts, such as Apple Strudel with Warm Cider Sauce, Apricot and Orange Fool, and Raspberry Creams. Tropical Fruit Salad is a simple and refreshing dessert, dressed with your choice of fresh fruit juice. You will find that all these recipes will bring an enjoyable finale to any meal.

puddings
& desserts

golden baked apple pudding

very easy   serves 4

15 minutes   30–35 minutes

ingredients

450 g/1 lb cooking apples

1 tsp ground cinnamon

2 tbsp sultanas

115 g/4 oz wholemeal bread

125 g/4½ oz low-fat cottage cheese

4 tbsp soft light brown sugar

250 ml/9 fl oz semi-skimmed milk

NUTRITIONAL INFORMATION	
calories	227
protein	5 g
carbohydrate	52 g
sugars	40 g
fat	2 g
saturates	1 g

Preheat the oven to 220°C/425°F/Gas Mark 7.

Peel and core the apples and chop the flesh into 1-cm/½-inch pieces. Put in a bowl and toss with the cinnamon and sultanas.

Remove the crusts and cut the bread into 1-cm/½-inch cubes. Add to the apples with the cottage cheese and 3 tablespoons of the brown sugar and mix together. Stir in the milk.

Turn the mixture into an ovenproof dish and sprinkle with the remaining sugar. Bake in the oven for 30–35 minutes, or until golden brown. Serve hot.

apricot & orange fool

extremely easy

serves 4

5 minutes

ingredients

250 g/9 oz ready-to-eat dried apricots

1 tbsp clear honey

250 ml/9 fl oz fresh orange juice

250 ml/9 fl oz low-fat natural yogurt

2 tsp flaked almonds (toasted), to decorate

NUTRITIONAL INFORMATION	
calories	171
protein	6 g
carbohydrate	37 g
sugars	37 g
fat	1 g
saturates	0 g

Put all the ingredients, except the almonds, in a food processor and blend until smooth.

Serve in individual glass dishes, decorated with toasted almonds.

spiced baked pears

extremely easy

serves 4

5 minutes

30 minutes

4 large, firm eating pears
150 ml/5 fl oz apple juice
1 cinnamon stick

4 whole cloves
1 bay leaf

NUTRITIONAL INFORMATION	
calories	114
protein	1 g
carbohydrate	29 g
sugars	29 g
fat	0 g
saturates	0 g

Preheat the oven to 180°C/350°F/Gas Mark 4.

Peel and core the pears and cut them into quarters. Place in an ovenproof dish and add the remaining ingredients.

Cover the dish and bake in the oven for 30 minutes.

Serve the pears hot or cold.

apple strudel with warm cider sauce

easy   serves 2–4

25 minutes   15–20
minutes

ingredients

8 crisp eating apples
1 tbsp lemon juice
85 g/3 oz sultanas
1 tsp ground cinnamon
½ tsp grated nutmeg
1 tbsp soft light brown sugar
6 sheets filo pastry
vegetable oil spray

SAUCE
1 tbsp cornflour
450 ml/16 fl oz cider

icing sugar, to serve

NUTRITIONAL INFORMATION	
calories	283
protein	3 g
carbohydrate	61 g
sugars	47 g
fat	1 g
saturates	0 g

Preheat the oven to 190°C/375°F/Gas Mark 5. Line a baking sheet with non-stick liner.

Peel and core the apples and chop them into 1-cm/½-inch dice. Toss the pieces in a bowl with the lemon juice, sultanas, cinnamon, nutmeg and sugar.

Lay out a sheet of filo, spray with vegetable oil and lay a second sheet on top. Repeat with a third sheet. Spread over half the apple mixture and roll up lengthways, tucking in the ends to enclose the filling. Repeat to make a second strudel. Slide onto the baking sheet, spray with oil and bake for 15–20 minutes.

Blend the cornflour in a pan with a little cider until smooth. Add the remaining cider and heat gently, stirring all the time, until the mixture boils and thickens. Serve the strudel warm or cold, dredged with icing sugar and accompanied by the cider sauce.

tropical fruit salad

very easy   serves 4

20 minutes   none
+ 1 hour to
chill

1 ripe mango
1 papaya
1 small pineapple

300 ml/10 fl oz pineapple or orange juice
2 small bananas

NUTRITIONAL INFORMATION	
calories	154
protein	2 g
carbohydrate	38 g
sugars	37 g
fat	1 g
saturates	0 g

Cutting close to the stone, cut a large slice from one side of the mango, then cut another slice from the opposite side. Without breaking the skin, cut the flesh in the segments into squares, then push the skin inside out to expose the cubes and cut away from the skin. Use a sharp knife to peel the remaining centre section and cut the flesh away from the stone into cubes. Reserve any juice and put in a serving bowl with the mango flesh.

Cut the papaya in half and discard the seeds. Remove the skin and cut the flesh into cubes. Peel the pineapple, remove the centre core and as many 'eyes' as possible and cut the flesh into chunks. Add both fruits to the mango.

Pour over the fruit juice and chill the mixture in the refrigerator for about 1 hour. Just before serving, slice the bananas and add the slices to the fruit salad.

apple & honey water ice

very easy · serves 4

10 minutes
+ 5–6 hours
to freeze

20 minutes

ingredients

4 crisp eating apples
2 tbsp lemon juice
200 ml/7 fl oz + 1 tbsp water

5 tbsp sugar
2 tbsp clear honey

apple slices, to garnish

NUTRITIONAL INFORMATION	
calories	175
protein	0 g
carbohydrate	46 g
sugars	46 g
fat	0 g
saturates	0 g

Peel and core the apples and cut them into chunks. Put in a saucepan with the lemon juice and 1 tablespoon of water and heat gently for about 20 minutes, stirring frequently, until soft.

Meanwhile, put the sugar and 200 ml/7 fl oz water in a saucepan and heat gently, stirring, until dissolved. Bring to the boil, then boil for 2 minutes. Remove from the heat.

Push the apple through a sieve into a bowl. Stir in the sugar syrup and honey. Leave until cold.

When cold, pour the mixture into a freezer container. Freeze uncovered for 2 hours until the water ice mixture begins to set. Turn the mixture into a bowl and whisk until smooth. Return to the container and freeze for a further 3–4 hours until firm.

Serve garnished with apple slices.

raspberry creams

very easy   serves 4

10 minutes   none
+ 1 hour
to chill

450 g/1 lb raspberries
175 g/6 oz low-fat cottage cheese
3 tbsp sugar
150 ml/5 fl oz low-fat natural yogurt

icing sugar, to decorate

NUTRITIONAL INFORMATION	
calories	142
protein	9 g
carbohydrate	25 g
sugars	25 g
fat	1 g
saturates	1 g

Reserving a few whole raspberries to decorate, use the back of a spoon to push the raspberries and cottage cheese through a sieve into a bowl.

Stir the sugar and yogurt into the raspberry mixture and stir to blend, then spoon into individual serving dishes. Chill in the refrigerator for about 1 hour.

Serve chilled, decorated with the reserved raspberries and dusted with sifted icing sugar.

compôte of dried fruit

extremely
easy

serves 4

25 minutes
+ 24 hours
to marinate

ingredients

1 tbsp jasmine tea
300 ml/10 fl oz boiling water
55 g/2 oz dried apricots

55 g/2 oz dried apple rings
55 g/ 2oz dried prunes
300 ml/10 fl oz fresh orange juice

NUTRITIONAL INFORMATION	
calories	103
protein	2 g
carbohydrate	25 g
sugars	25 g
fat	0 g
saturates	0 g

Put the tea in a jug and pour over the boiling water. Leave to infuse for 20 minutes, then strain.

Put the dried fruits in a serving bowl and pour over the tea and orange juice. Cover and leave to marinate in the refrigerator for 24 hours.

Serve the compôte well chilled.

index